LOOK AND MAKE

KT-555-597

PRESENTS

W

FRANKLIN WATTS

LONDON • SYDNEY

Getting ready

Before you start making your presents, read all the instructions carefully and check that you have everything you need.

On the opposite page you can see the general things you will need. You can find these around your home or in most stationery shops.

Be prepared

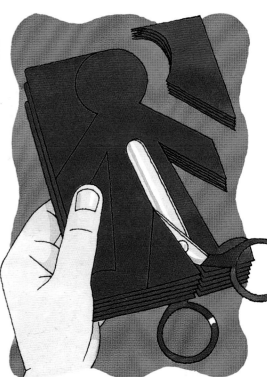

Cover your work area with plenty of old newspaper. Wear an apron or an old shirt and roll up your sleeves.

When you have finished, rinse your brushes and put the tops back on your felt-tip pens.

Be very careful when using scissors. If you find anything tricky to cut, ask an adult to help you.

You will need

Here are the things you will need most often when you make the presents in this book.

ready-mix paint

round-ended scissors

ribbon

coloured stiff paper

ruler

glue stick

felt-tip pens

PVA glue

pencils

paintbrushes

tissue paper

Animal bookmarks

You will need:

coloured stiff paper

glue stick

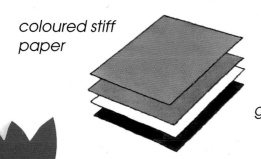

These would make an excellent present for a bookworm.

Try making other animal bookmarks.

Octopus

1.

Draw an octopus with long tentacles. Copy this one.

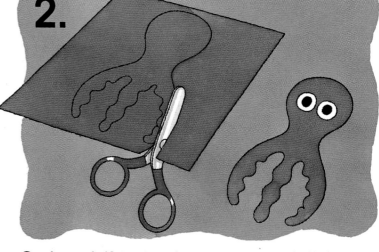

2.

Cut out the octopus carefully. Add big eyes.

Elephant

1.

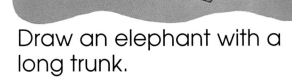

Draw an elephant with a long trunk.

2.

Cut around the elephant. Cut slits either side of its trunk. Add eyes.

Slide your bookmark over a page in a book.

Bright beads

You will need:

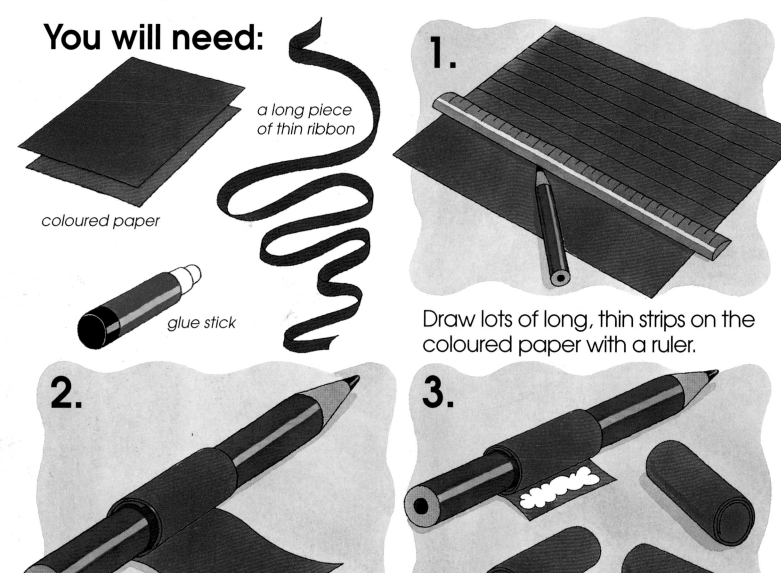

a long piece of thin ribbon

coloured paper

glue stick

1.

Draw lots of long, thin strips on the coloured paper with a ruler.

2.

Cut along the lines. Roll one of the strips around a pencil.

3.

Glue down the edge of the strip. Now carefully slide out the pencil.

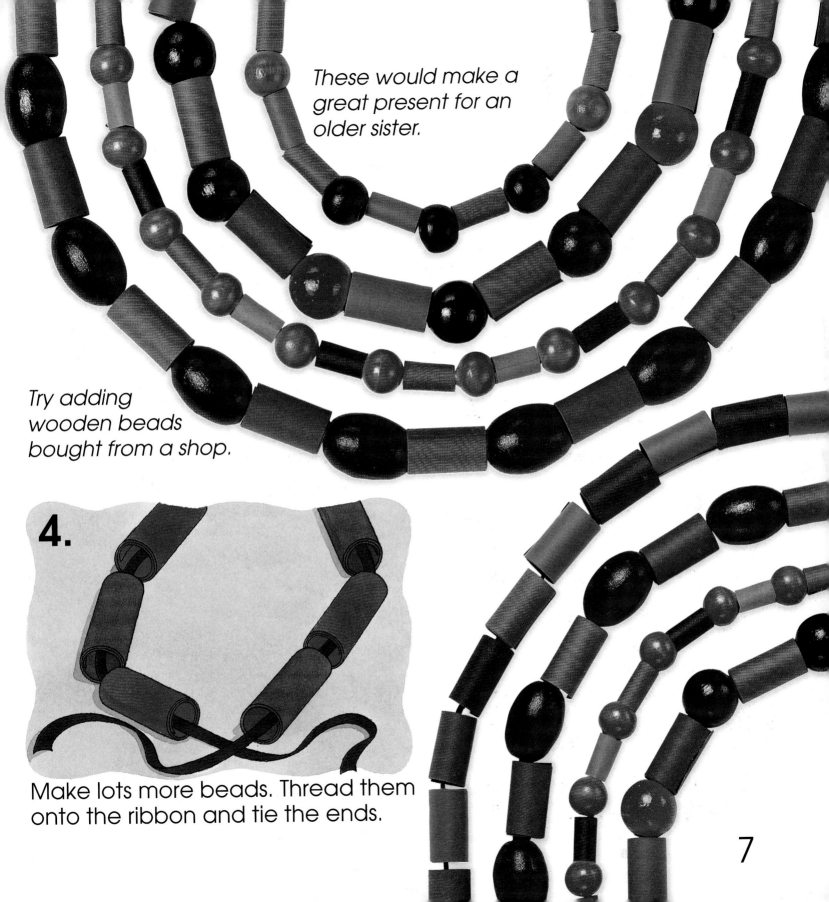

These would make a great present for an older sister.

Try adding wooden beads bought from a shop.

4.

Make lots more beads. Thread them onto the ribbon and tie the ends.

Hanging flowers

You will need:

coloured tissue paper

paper plate

sticky tape

two long ribbons

glue stick

coloured stiff paper

This flower would make a great present for Mother's Day.

1.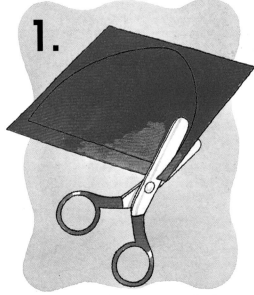

Draw a large petal shape like this on the stiff paper. Cut it out.

2.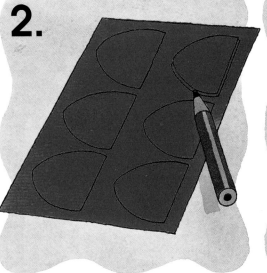

Draw round the petal six times. Cut out all the petals.

3.

Stick the petals to the back of the paper plate as shown here.

4.

Tear the tissue paper into squares and scrunch them up tightly into balls.

5.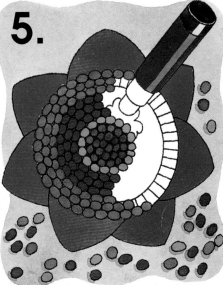

Stick the balls to the front of the plate. Use lots of colours. Cover the whole plate.

6.

Tape one end of each ribbon to the back of the plate. Tie the ends.

9

Starry stationery

You will need:

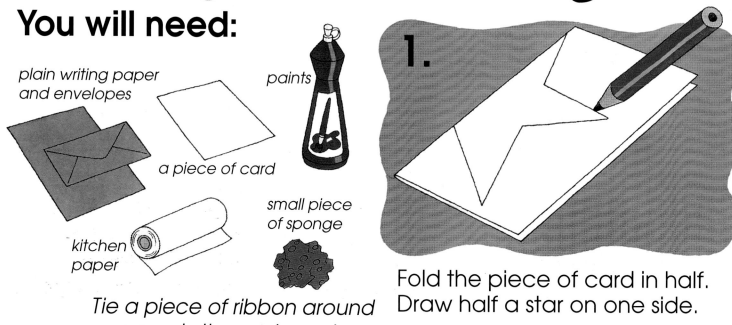

plain writing paper
and envelopes

paints

a piece of card

kitchen
paper

small piece
of sponge

*Tie a piece of ribbon around
your stationery to make a
lovely present.*

1.

Fold the piece of card in half.
Draw half a star on one side.

Try some other shapes.

2.

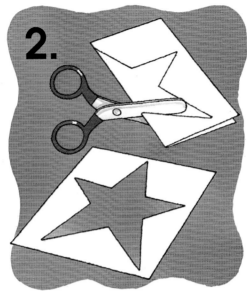

Cut the star out through both sides. Open the card out to make your stencil.

3.

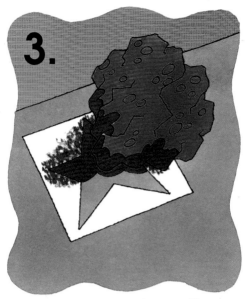

Hold your stencil firmly on your writing paper. Dab on paint with the sponge.

4.

Carefully lift off your stencil. Wipe it dry with the kitchen paper to use it again.

Decorate your envelopes in the same way.

Paper vase

You will need:

coloured paper

PVA glue

old cup (to mix the glue in)

water

old jar (or glass)

paintbrush

Fill your vase with flowers to make a beautiful present.

1.

Cut or tear lots of different coloured pieces of paper.

2.

Mix some glue with a little water and stir with the paintbrush.

3.

Stick the pieces of paper to the jar with the watery glue.

4.

The glue is clear when dry.

Varnish the jar with PVA glue. Then leave it to dry.

Clown frieze

You will need:

a long piece of coloured stiff paper

glue stick

scraps of coloured paper

ruler

Ask an adult to stick your frieze to your baby brother or sister's bedroom wall.

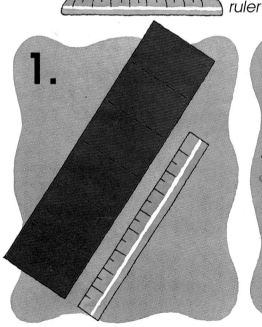

1.

Divide the long piece of paper into six equal parts with the ruler and pencil.

2.

Fold the paper back and forth along the lines to make a fan shape.

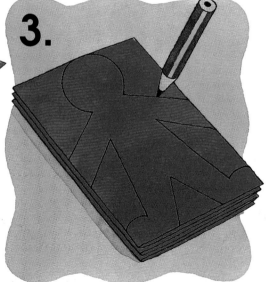

3.

Draw a clown shape on the top fold. Make sure its hands and feet touch the edges.

14

4. Cut around the clown. Then open the paper out to make a chain of clowns.

5. Decorate the clowns with paper hats, eyes, bow ties, buttons and anything else you like.

15

Desk tidy

This will make a useful present for an untidy person!

You will need:

thick piece of cardboard

paints

PVA glue

saucer (to draw round for the base)

round objects (use spraycan lids, toilet roll tubes, cheese boxes)

1.

Ask an adult to help.

Draw a circle on the cardboard and cut it out to make the base.

2.

Paint the base and the round objects with thick paint.

3.

Leave to dry. Then glue the objects to the base.

17

Tissue eggs

You will need:

one or more eggs

PVA glue

scraps of coloured tissue paper

small bowl

thick needle

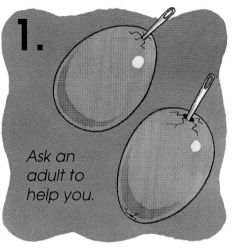

1.

Ask an adult to help you.

Make a small hole in the pointed end of the egg and a larger hole in the other.

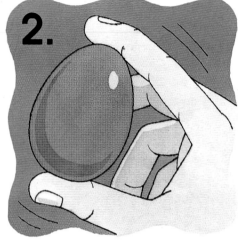

2.

Put your finger and thumb over the holes. Then gently shake the egg.

3.

Blow hard into the small hole. Shake the egg and blow again until it is empty.

4.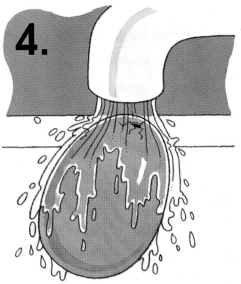

Rinse the egg under the tap. Blow through the bigger hole and wipe the egg dry.

5. *The tissue paper will cover any cracks.*

Glue scraps of tissue paper to the egg. Smooth them down gently with your fingers.

You could put your eggs in a basket, filled with tissue paper.

6. *The glue is clear when dry.*

Cover the egg with tissue. Leave to dry. Then varnish it with watery PVA glue.

19

Scrap book

You will need:

coloured stiff paper

coloured paper

pieces of ribbon (or string)

hole punch

1. Draw and cut out two rectangles of stiff paper both the same size to make the covers of the book.

2. Draw around one of the covers on some coloured paper.

3. Cut out the rectangle to make a page. Make lots of pages.

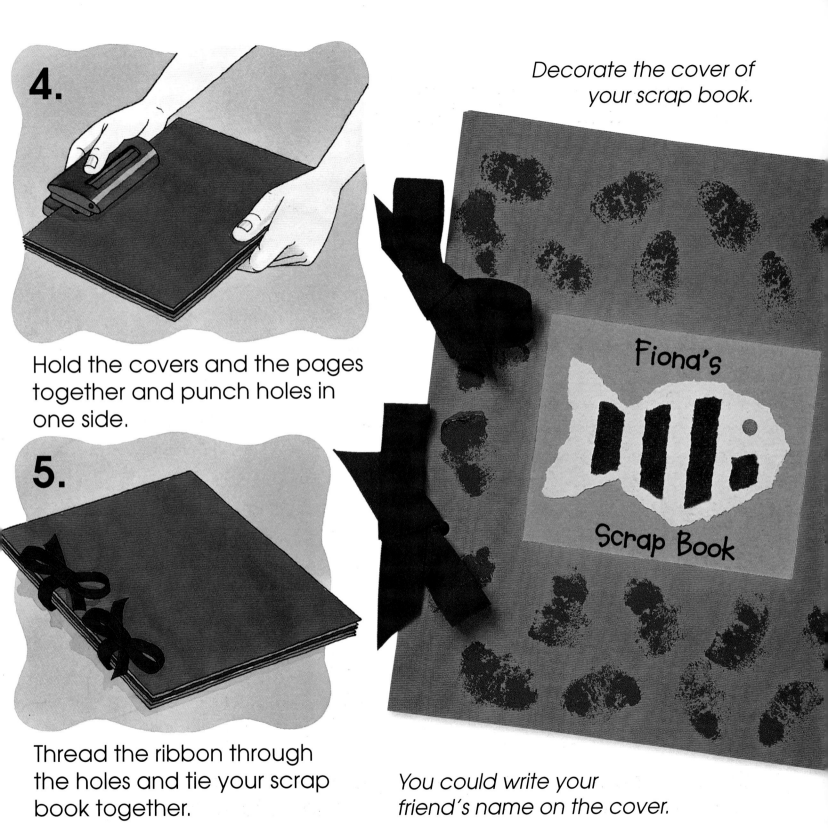

4.

Hold the covers and the pages together and punch holes in one side.

5.

Thread the ribbon through the holes and tie your scrap book together.

Decorate the cover of your scrap book.

Fiona's

Scrap Book

You could write your friend's name on the cover.

Name snake

You will need:

empty matchboxes (one for each letter of your friend's name and one extra for the head)

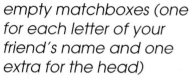

glue stick

short strips of ribbon

coloured paper

felt-tip pen

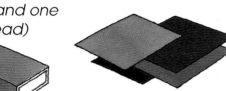

sticky tape

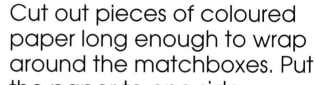
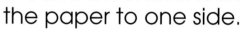

1.

Cut out pieces of coloured paper long enough to wrap around the matchboxes. Put the paper to one side.

Add red paper stripes.

22

2.

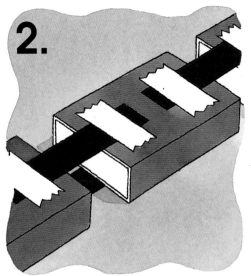

3.

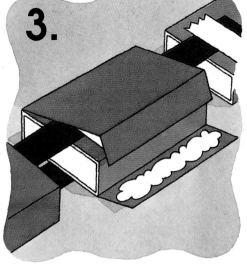

4.

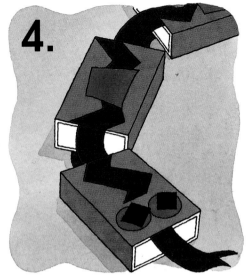

Join the matchboxes together by taping the strips of ribbon on the tops and bottoms.

Wrap the coloured paper around each matchbox and glue down the edge.

Decorate your snake. Add eyes, a tongue and paper squares to write on.

This would make a fun present for a friend. Write their name in the letter squares.

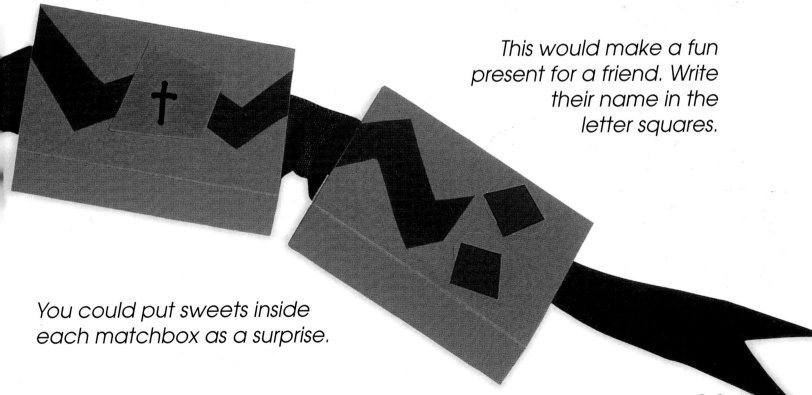

You could put sweets inside each matchbox as a surprise.

Pencil aliens

You will need:

pen

smart pencils

PVA glue

sponge cloths

1. Put the end of a pencil on a piece of cloth. Draw an alien face around it and cut it out.

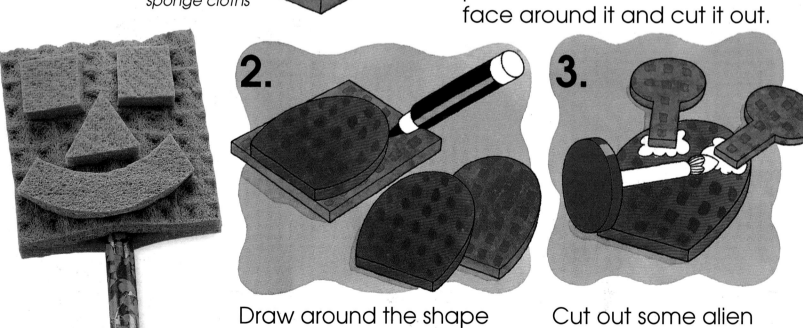

2. Draw around the shape onto another cloth and cut out a second face.

3. Cut out some alien ears. Glue them onto one face shape.

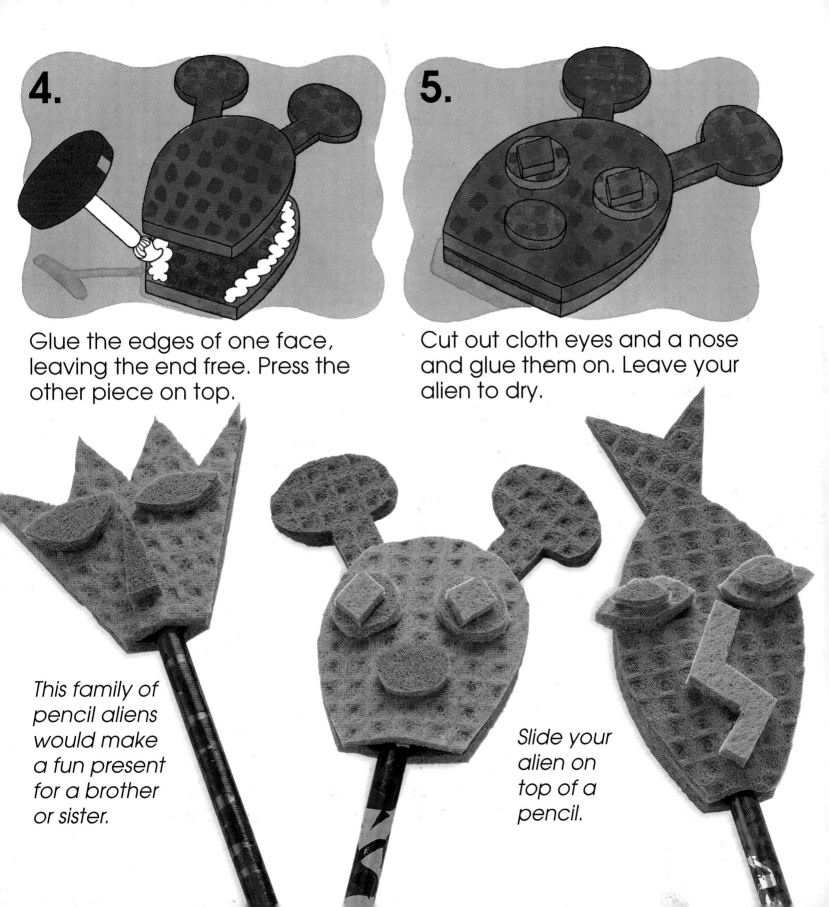

4. Glue the edges of one face, leaving the end free. Press the other piece on top.

5. Cut out cloth eyes and a nose and glue them on. Leave your alien to dry.

This family of pencil aliens would make a fun present for a brother or sister.

Slide your alien on top of a pencil.

Footie key-ring

You will need:

baking tray

wire cooling rack

thin ribbon

acrylic paints

wooden spoon

rolling pin

2 cups of salt

1 cup of warm water

knife

mixing bowl

2 cups of plain flour, plus a little extra

PVA glue

1.

Mix the flour, salt and warm water together in the bowl.

Before you start, set your oven to 150°C/ 300°F/ gas mark 2.

Line your baking tray with foil.

2.

Cover your fingers with flour. Mix and squeeze the mixture with your hands until it forms a soft ball of dough.

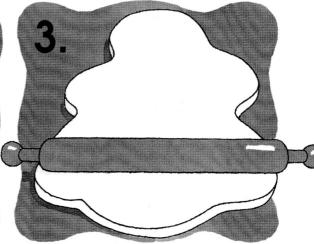

3.

Sprinkle flour on a surface and the rolling pin. Roll out the dough until it is about as thick as a pencil.

4.

Cut a circle from the dough.
Use a glass to cut around.
Make a hole near the edge.

5.

*See the box in the bottom left.
Ask an adult to help.*

Bake the dough
for about an hour.
Leave it to cool.

*This will make a
great present for
your dad.*

*Try making a car
key-ring.*

6.

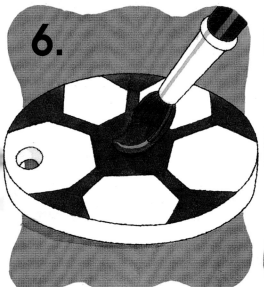

Paint on football
colours. Let it dry.
Then paint it again
and leave it to dry.

7.

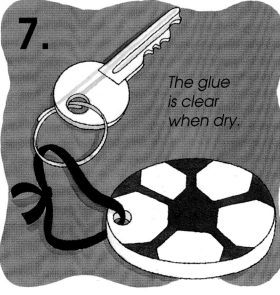

*The glue
is clear
when dry.*

Paint the football with PVA
glue to varnish it. Let it dry.
Thread the ribbon through
the hole and tie it to a key.

27

Wrapping paper

You will need:

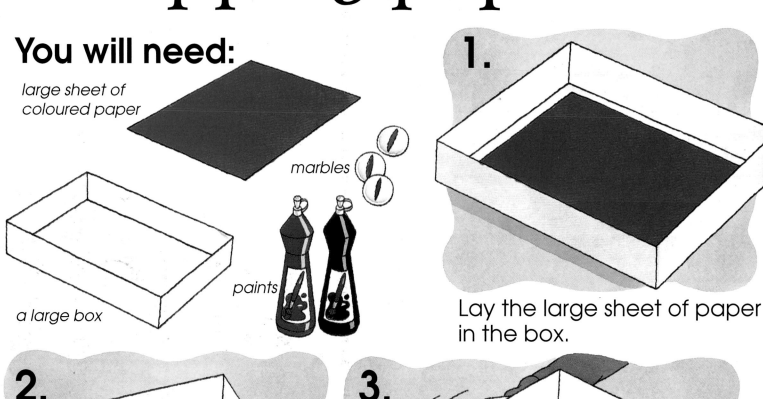

large sheet of
coloured paper

marbles

paints

a large box

1.

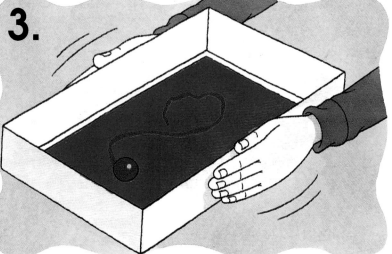

Lay the large sheet of paper in the box.

2.

Roll one of the marbles in some watery paint. Then place it on the paper.

3.

Gently tilt the box from side to side to make the marble roll about and make a pattern.

Try flicking paint from a paintbrush onto your paper for a different effect.

4.

Take the marble out and repeat steps 2 and 3 with different colours.

Gift wrapping

You will need:

a present in a box

wrapping paper

sticky tape

1.

Cut a piece of wrapping paper longer and wider than the present.

Tie a big ribbon around your present.

Turn the page to see how to make the gift tags.

2.

Fold the wrapping paper over the present as shown. Tape down the top edge.

3.

Tuck down one end of the paper. Fold in the flaps on each side so that they form a point.

4.

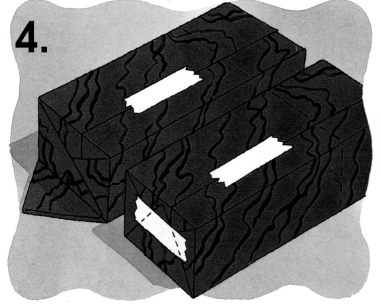

Stick the pointed flap of paper to the side of the present with sticky tape.

5.

Turn the present around and repeat steps 3 and 4 for the other end of the present.

Jazzy gift tags

You will need:

a small piece of stiff paper

hole punch (or a pencil point)

wool (or thin ribbon)

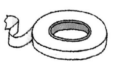
sticky tape

1.

Draw a bell shape on the paper. Cut it out and punch a hole in the top.

2.

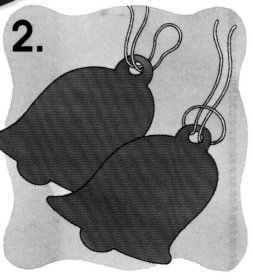

Make as many gift tags as you need.

Thread the wool through the hole as shown.

3.

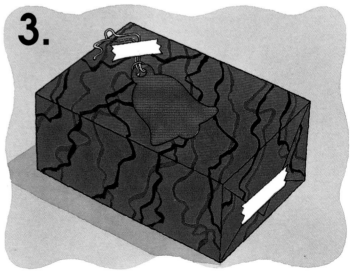

Write your message on one side of the tag and stick it to the present.

32